IT'S ALL ABOUT APATHY

GAME PLAN YOUR NEXT MOVE

MICHAEL GONZALES

a LEADERSHIP BOOK

It's All About Apathy

© 2021 Michael Gonzales

ALL RIGHTS RESERVED. Any unauthorized reprint or use of this material is prohibited. No part of this book may be reproduced or transmitted in any form or by any means, electronic or mechanical, including photocopying, recording, or by any information storage and retrieval system, without express written permission from the author/publisher.

A friend challenged me to write and publish a book in 30 days.

This is the result.

Table of **Contents**

Preface 2
Making Moves 5
Kaizen 14
Chance Favors the Prepared 21
Be A Leader, Not A Boss 29
Delayed Gratification 40
Just Start Now 46

AP·A·THY *noun*

Definition: lack of interest, enthusiasm, or concern

'widespread apathy among leaders'

Michael Gonzales

Preface

Disclaimer: I'm not a writer or storyteller; however, I wrote this book because I wanted to share a few principles that have helped me improve my business, flourish my relationships, and finesse my leadership skills. This short book aims to remove **apathy** from your life by creating actionable game plans to help you become a better decision-maker and inspirational leader. The purpose of this book is to help leaders step outside of their comfort zone to get things done, accomplish their goals, and lead others well.

It wasn't very long ago when I was a young college student trying to figure out what I wanted to do in life. I didn't know what career path I would take, let alone what a career path even was. There was a period in my life where I became unmotivated and apathetic simply because I felt like I couldn't get ahead in life. From my perspective, my classmates, friends, and everyone else around me seemed to have everything together and figured out. I had classmates studying medicine to become successful doctors. I had friends traveling all over the world and exploring exciting new places. I had people in my life constantly asking me about my plans and my passions, and I pretended I knew how to answer their questions. In reality, I had no idea what I was doing. I didn't know what direction to take or what to do with my future. I was simply going through the motions and doing pretty much what ever my peers were doing. In my head, everyone was already successful or about to be, and everyone had everything figured. I was terrified of being found out, and I had no clue what my next move would be, so I would pretend like I knew what I was doing. I would fake it until I made it because I knew I wanted to be successful one day. The bad news is, this type of thinking can lead to apathy and spin you into a cycle of carelessness and living for the now. Apathy is not caring and lacking motivation in life. And if you don't want to do anything, then take the apathetic approach and just do nothing. However, if you're ready to make some moves, keep reading. I'll share a few stories and action steps to get you inspired and moving forward. At the end of each chapter, I'll include practical action items to challenge and help game plan your next move. Let's go ahead and make some moves!

It's All About Apathy

CHAPTER ONE

Making Moves

The summer of 2007 marked many moments of transition for me. I had just graduated from high school in Orange County, CA and college was right around the corner. I was both excited and nervous. I was excited because this would be the first time I would be genuinely independent and live away from home. I was worried though because I knew my family and I were taking heavy student loans to pay for my private college tuition. I chose to attend Point Loma Nazarene University in sunny San Diego. The private university campus overlooked the beautiful Pacific Ocean and was home to about 3000 students. Part of the reason why I chose to attend this university was that it was close, but not too close to home. More importantly, it had a greater than 85% acceptance rate for pre-med students to get accepted into medical school and I wanted to be a doctor. Spoiler alert: I'm part of the failed 15% that does not make it. I went into college declaring my major as pre-medicine. I chose a medical career because I knew it was stable, prestigious, and let's face it, doctors make bank, baby! I knew it would be difficult, but I was determined. I knew I would be spending a lot of time in the library studying while all of the 'undeclared' majors were out having fun and partying. It was a sacrifice I was willing to make though because I knew if I stuck with it long enough, and put in enough work, I would be successful.

    The problems started to come when I wasn't getting the desired results in my classes. The amount of time and effort I put into studying for my science exams were not an accurate representation of my grades; however, I was determined to be successful. Over the next several years, I didn't miss any classes, and I studied meticulously for every exam. I learned both alone, and with my fellow peers, and participated in any extra credit given after class. I put in the hours and work, but something didn't click whenever I took a test. I didn't get bad grades per se. I never failed a class, and I had a mixture of mostly B's and C's; however, the grades did not reflect the amount of work I was putting into studying. Grades of B's and C's are not bad by any means, but I was trying to become a doctor, and quite frankly, with those grades, I would not get into medical school.

During my junior year of college, I decided to call it quits with medicine. I officially became part of the 15% of the Point Loma Nazarene University pre-med students who didn't cut it, and I had had enough! I ultimately made this decision because I knew I was on a path of not making it and it was causing me to be extremely unhappy. I was tired, discouraged, and devastated. By far, my most significant panic and worry was I had spent (borrowed via loan) nearly $65,000 on college tuition, all for nothing. "How was I going to pay it all back?" I thought to myself. I knew I had to make some moves, so I decided to study abroad! Wait, what?!

After the decision to study abroad, I became a little apathetic. I just didn't care as much about school anymore. A big reason I decided to study abroad was that most of my pre-med friends were doing it. However, they had better grades than I did and were on track to accomplish their goals. Whereas, I had just dropped out of pre-med and decided it was all about apathy, and I was going to have some fun.

In 2009, I traveled and studied abroad in Seville, Spain. I spent the next semester making new friends, exploring the city, and traveling to neighboring countries. I had a blast, but my time in Seville was quick. Before I knew it, I was back in San Diego with little idea of what I would do and was still majorly in debt.

    I decided to continue college and switched my major to business administration. I didn't know what business administration meant, but it sounded like something I could easily finish with unlimited possibilities. One class I took was called "Business Communication", which taught me how to write effective resumes and communicate well. Little did I know at the time that this class would inevitably spark a change of trajectory in my life with one single assignment.

Do something uncomfortable. Step so far outside of your comfort zone and become a better version of you.

    For this one assignment, I was asked to conduct 'informational interviews.' An informational interview is a practice of interviewing people of great power and success, such as C-level executives, business owners, and decision-makers. An informational interview aims to learn about the person's story, their industry, and build a relationship with that person. I took the challenge head on, and I mustered up the courage to research and call local business owners in San Diego. Once I got them on the phone, I asked if I could buy them a cup of coffee for 15 minutes of their time so I could pick their brain. After leaving many unanswered voicemails and receiving the answer "No," I quickly learned the difficulty of contacting these business owners. Regardless, I continued to call until I had success, and I conducted my first set of interviews. With each interview, I learned more of real-world business practices and strategies. Still, beyond that, I was able to get out of my comfort zone, face rejection well, and make moves. This greatly enhanced my confidence and improved my communication ability with others. I learned how to ask the right questions, and each interviewee made me feel important, growing my faith. Without knowing, I began to enjoy taking on challenges and welcoming opposition like an old friend. I became encouraged, motivated, and, most importantly, excited to make moves again!

The Game Plan: Your Turn To Make Moves

Action Item: *Conduct informational interviews. This is an intimidating exercise, however, this may change your life. Follow these steps.*

Research, Call & Email, Don't Give Up!

1.) Research *Be as detailed and specific as possible*
- Google ten local business owners, executives, leaders in your local area that you're interested in.
- Research and learn as much as you can about them online.
- Jot down a few questions about their story or their company that interests you. For example, you may be interested in knowing why they chose the industry they are in or how they got started.
- Find all and any contact information. This can be the main business telephone number, email address, or even a LinkedIn profile.
- Lastly, Google the address of the closest coffee shop to their business or office.

2.) Call & Email *Practice. Practice. Practice.*

- Now that you're done researching, it is time to pick up the phone and call. This is scary, but the practice of this is so worth it.
- Get in contact with them by phone. If you are calling the main business line, be polite and honest and tell the gatekeeper you would like to interview the owner/leader to ask questions about their story and passions for their business.
- If they do not pick up, leave a voicemail and send a follow up email.
- You may use the phone script below, however, feel free to modify and make it sound more like *you*.
    - "Hi [leaders name], my name is [your name]. I saw your website and was interested in [area of interest], I wanted to know if I could buy you a cup of coffee at [local coffee shop] across the street from your office at [say street address of office] and pick your brain for 15 minutes."

3.) Don't Give Up *You can do this!*

- This is the most important part. Don't give up! You will get rejected a lot and that is completely normal. Remember, view rejection as growth and it will make you strong.
- Repeat this process. The more you practice, the better and more confident you will be.
- This is hard and most people will skip this action item. However, you will be surprised at how many influential leaders say "Yes" to your request and are more than happy to help.
- Remember, this process may change your life and be the beginning of a new opportunity.

Kaizen

CHAPTER TWO

Kaizen

The summer after I graduated college, I got a job as a Business Development Specialist for an information technology company in San Diego. Business development is just a fancy way of saying I had a sales career. A big part of my role was to gain new customers. Any job in sales is difficult because you deal with cold calling down a long list of potential customers and facing a lot of rejection. During my day, I would spend hours researching potential customers, developing a call list, and making calls to set an appointment with a customer. This process became grueling, day in and day out. However, it taught me the importance of having tenacity and developing the ability to overcome difficult situations. I was fortunate to have this job because the founder of the company, Jim, became a sort of entrepreneurial mentor to me. Jim was passionate about business, leadership, and helping others grow. He taught me how to make better decisions, strengthen my communication, and always seek to improve. He would often take time coaching and leading his team with invaluable skills to better create a more robust culture.

During one of Jim's coaching sessions, he introduced us to *Kaizen* (**kai** · zn). Kaizen is a Japanese business principle meaning: continuous improvement. The idea is to always improve, no matter how small, every day. Jim challenged our team to be aware and seek out areas in both our business and personal lives to make a slight improvement.

Being in business development, I spent much of the day sitting at a desk, researching potential clients, and making phone calls. As you can imagine, sitting at a desk all day can create desk fatigue and poor posture. I noticed there was an exercise ball at the office not in use, so I decided to use it as my everyday chair to improve and bring more attention to my posture. This small improvement of switching an ordinary desk chair with an exercise ball made significant benefits to my posture over time. It is also an excellent example of Kaizen, where a small change can substantially impact you over time. Never underestimate the power of tiny gains.

Imagine you can improve one habit by one percent every day for one year. Where would you be by the end of the year? More importantly, what specific habits in your life would you want to change or improve over the year? If you are struggling with this decision, take comfort in knowing that it is normal to feel overwhelmed as you step out of apathy and into intentional living. We will never run out of areas in our life to grow and improve in. Although it can be challenging, it is better to not waste time overthinking which area to choose, but instead simply choose one so that you can begin the practice of Kaizen.

"Continuous improvement is better than delayed perfection" - Mark Twain

While working in sales, I often struggled with both cold calling and public speaking. Unfortunately, these were necessary skills to have in order to be successful in sales. After countless call rejections and failures to close the deal, the job became monotonous, and I was not getting better or improving in any way. I felt I had too many work projects to complete and didn't have enough time in the day to execute and close deals. I felt stuck while trying to look for ways to apply Kaizen and make improvements. Fortunately, Jim introduced me to the SWOT analysis. He gave me a key piece of advice to get where I wanted to go; I needed to know where I stood. In essence, you can have all of your goals set. However, if you do not know where you stand or your starting point, it is tough to reach your goals. This advice is universal and even works when giving directions. Imagine a friend calls you and asks you for directions to Los Angeles, California. Your friend, however, does not know where he is located. It would be complicated for you to give proper advice. This same principle applies to your goals. If you want to improve and reach your goals, it is essential to know where you stand, and the SWOT analysis will help you determine that.

The SWOT analysis is an acronym that helps you identify your Strengths, Weaknesses, Opportunities, and Threats. This tool can be applied to your life, business, or even a particular situation to help you plan and create decisive actions. Strengths and weaknesses are internal factors, which typically you can directly control. Opportunities and threats are external factors that may influence your situation. I created a SWOT analysis and began identifying the strengths, weaknesses, opportunities, and threats of my sales role. After completing the SWOT analysis, I created specific action items to combat each deficiency. For example, one weakness I identified was being impatient and constantly having the need to get things done immediately when assigned a task, even if the quality of my work would suffer. I created an action item to combat this weakness by setting focused time on my digital calendar to execute the next actions when assigned a work task. As a result, I had dedicated time to complete projects while also having more than enough time to plan, prepare, and execute my cold call sessions and generate appointments with clients. And later in the year, I won a sales contest for an all-expense-paid trip to Cabo San Lucas! Just remember, you must know where you are to reach your goals. So, go on to create a SWOT analysis of your life!

The Game Plan: **Practice Kaizen**

Action Item: *Create a SWOT Analysis of your life. Keep improving, you may just win a trip or prize at your job!*

Strengths, Weakness, Opportunities, Threats

1.) SWOT Analysis *Write it down*

- What are your internal Strengths in your life?
- What are your internal Weaknesses in your life?
- Which external Opportunities are affecting you?
- Which external Threats are affecting you?

2.) Combat Weakness *Write it down*

- For each weakness you listed, create a specific action item to combat it
- Take action now

SWOT ANALYSIS

STRENGTHS | WEAKNESSES

OPPORTUNITIES | THREATS

CHAPTER THREE

Chance Favors the Prepared

My favorite class in high school was Physics. I loved the course, not for science, but because the teacher, Mr. Spoonemore, shared memorable stories and taught simple principles to help you in life. The class setup was a lab setting with all the chairs and tables for the students in the middle of the room. Along the wall, computers were mounted for group projects. During the first Physics test of the year, we were given directions to complete the exam, turn it back into Mr. Spoonemore's desk, and walk back to our seats while waiting for the other students to complete their tests. When the last student walked up, turned in the exam, and sat back down, Mr. Spoonemore stood up and with a disappointing voice asked the entire class why no one used the computers to help them with their test. Our collective response was we assumed we weren't allowed to use the computers and thought it would be cheating (Hello, apathetic mindset!). He mentioned he never said we were not allowed, and if anyone used the computers to Google all of the answers for the first test, he would have allowed it. Sure enough, for the remainder of the year, Mr. Spoonemore prohibited using computers for following exams. He only allowed the use of computers for the first test when everyone assumed they were not allowed. "The lesson of the day is to proceed until apprehended," Mr. Spoonemore shouted. Those words were comical, however, they stuck with me. This taught me to always be on the lookout for unexpected opportunities. You see, apathy is not an action, but a mindset. If you aren't curious and constantly trying to make moves then it is easy to miss out on opportunities. It's easy to spot a blue car when you're always thinking about a blue car. In the same way, it is easy to spot an opportunity when you're only thinking about possibilities.

    March 8th, 2018, was the grand opening of my very own Chick-fil-A restaurant in National City, CA. Before the grand opening, I hired a team of 70 employees, identified future leaders, and facilitated leadership workshops to prepare our team and the business for a high-volume opening. I was ready, excited, and confident our grand opening team would execute well. And guess what?! They did FANTASTIC!

In many cases, when you start a brand new business, you will run in to many hiccups and unexpected challenges. We were lucky not to come across many major issues. Within three months of opening, the restaurant was not only self-sustainable, but growing at a high rate to become a market leader. Fast forward to one year later, our restaurant sales continued to grow, and the subsequent year sales grew by double digits. This type of growth is uncommon to put things in perspective in the fast-food restaurant industry. Chick-fil-A as a whole generates more revenue per unit compared to any other fast food restaurant in the entire world. And we are closed on Sundays.

How is Chick-fil-A able to maintain this growth? How is this even possible with only being open six days a week? Maybe we just got lucky. Or perhaps chance favors the prepared.

I started working at Chick-fil-A in 2014. I started as a team member with the intention to one day own and operate my very own Chick-fil-A franchise. As a team member, part of my goal was to learn all of the aspects of business operations, from restaurant cleaning/maintenance to legal processes. I did everything from scrubbing floors and cleaning toilets to handling orders and serving guests. At every opportunity, I would seek to understand

and learn every small detail on how the restaurant operates, from how our HVAC system works to our relationships with vendors and suppliers. I did this because I wanted to be 100% prepared for an unexpected opportunity with Chick-fil-A.

A few years later, I had the opportunity to work for Chick-fil-A corporate headquartered in Atlanta, Georgia. My role under corporate was to partner with local franchise owners and help open their brand new Chick-fil-A restaurants. For two years, I lived out of a hotel and lived in a new city every three months. By the end of two years, I helped open 9 Chick-fil-A restaurants in 9 different cities across the United States. I made sure I was purpose-driven at each restaurant I helped open. I set out to learn the best practices and wisdom from each opening, and each franchise owner, to better prepare myself to excel in future opportunities.

Proper Preparation Prevents Poor Performance

When I had the opportunity to open my very own Chick-fil-A restaurant, I was extremely confident in its operational success. A big contributor to my confidence was my preparation for this moment. I had spent many years learning about the best practices and scenarios to efficiently run operations, hire and develop top-level talent, and create a culture geared toward long-term success. Little did I know at the time, my Chick-fil-A restaurant would grow to be one of the highest volume restaurants within the Chick-fil-A chain. Some of our success may be luck, but remember, chance favors the prepared. In most situations, the more prepared you are, the more successful you become.

    Let's end this chapter with goal setting and creating action items specific to your goals. Remember, the more work you put into your dreams, the likelier you are to achieve them. You may even find some unexpected opportunities, if you're watching for them!

The Game Plan: Prepare Your Goals

Action Item: *Create specific goals and achieve them*

Always prepare. You might get lucky!

1.) Mind Dump Your Goals Write it down

- On a blank sheet of paper, write down every goal you have or want to achieve. You paper should look messy and full of goals.

2.) Narrow Down Choose

- Narrow down your goals and choose only two goals you want to achieve: one personal and one professional.

3.) Make Your Goals SMART Make it simple

- Make your goals [specific, measurable, achievable, relevant, time bound]
    - Is your goal Specific?
    - Is your goal Measurable?
    - Is your goal Achievable?
    - Is your goal Relevant to you?
    - Is your goal Time-Bound?

Example Goal vs SMART Goal

Goal: I want to go workout everyday.

SMART Goal Questions:

- Specific? Work out strength and cardio.
- Measurable? Work out six days a week.
- Achievable? Workout strength training for 30 minutes on Monday, Wednesday, and Friday. Workout cardio for 30 minutes Tuesday, Thursday, Saturday. Sundays off.
- Relevant? Workouts are important to me because it keeps me healthy and full of energy.
- Time-Bound? I'll commit to this work out routine the entire month of April.

SMART GOAL: My workout routine for the entire month of April will consist of Strength Training on Monday, Wednesday, Friday and Cardio Workout on Tuesday, Thursday, Saturday. Sundays are my day off.

It's All About Apathy

CHAPTER FOUR

Be A Leader, Not A Boss

Leadership happens everywhere, whether you know it or not. It occurs within organizations, businesses, and social settings among friends. Leadership occurs whenever people are around. In this chapter, we will explore the difference between a leader and a boss and share a few tips on becoming a leader who can create trust, buy-in, and be an inspiration for the people around them.

Often, individuals seek to become leaders or bosses within their organizations to gain social significance or wealth. However, it is essential to understand the difference between the two in order to lead others well. Let's paint a picture of a boss vs. leader.

When I think of a boss, I think of a person who leads from behind. This person commands and expects the members of his/her team to complete all the work. Frequently, when the team meets the work, it is the boss who takes the credit and recognition for a job well done. When the team fails, the boss defers and places blame on the team members. A boss generally does not create a sense of safety and trust within their workplace or employees. Bosses tend to be very "me" centered.

On the flip side, a leader leads from the very front and works side by side with his/her team. The leader and the team work together to complete tasks. When results are a success, everyone celebrates, and hefty credit is given to the team. When products are a failure, the leader takes ownership and accepts blame for the loss. A leader never expects their staff to do a job they themselves wouldn't do. A leader fosters a culture of trust and safety for their employees. Leaders are "we" centered.

Leader vs. Boss

Based on this example, who would you want to work for? Would you rather work for the boss or the leader? Better yet, who would you rather be: a boss or a leader? A boss takes an apathetic approach with their employees, whereas a leader is much more attentive. If you're goal is to be more intentional in your life, then I recommend adapting a servant leader mindset.

One thing I love is that Chick-fil-A is much more than a fast-food restaurant. It is more of a people company disguised as a quick-service restaurant. It is people who drive the business toward long-term success. Chick-fil-A focuses on several critical success factors; however, the top focus is people.

As a whole, Chick-fil-A has a balanced culture where people come before profits yet, at the same time, maintains a strong expectation for achievable business results. Chick-fil-A does a great job of balancing both people and business. Chick-fil-A is a business. It needs to generate revenue to maintain long-term financial and business success. Simultaneously, Chick-fil-A's number one asset is people, and by putting people first, Chick-fil-A has generated fantastic business results.

When I opened my Chick-fil-A restaurant in 2018, I started with a team of 70 team members. Due to strong and steady year-over-year sales increases, my restaurant doubled that number and grew to a total of 145 team members. In general, the fast-food industry is plagued with high employee turnover. We were fortunate to have a strong relational culture, which generates a high retention rate within our business. Our business's critical success is focusing on people and creating a culture where we put people first. So, what does it mean to focus on people?

To create a culture that is focused on relationship and people, you have to start from the top. We put people first by developing our leadership team first and foremost and by teaching them how to become servant leaders. A servant leader leads by example, encourages the group, seeks to understand others, develops other leaders, takes extreme ownership, and is teachable.

In our organization, a true leader has the following three characteristics. The first is INTEGRITY. Does this person do the right thing when no one is looking? The second is APTITUDE. Does this person have the ability to make decisions and teach decision-making even during challenging moments? The last is

CHEMISTRY. Can this person captivate, serve, and lead a team without leading by the title on their badge? By investing in our team and coaching them on leadership and the characteristics of having integrity, aptitude, and chemistry, we can develop strong leaders, creating a strong relational culture that is focused on the person in front of them.

      Creating a culture of transparency is vital. When it comes to raises, hours, and promotions at Chick-fil-A, we do not hand those out. They are always earned. We do not believe in participation awards, rather, we believe those who come in with a consistent work ethic, servant leader's attitude, and strong character are the people who will be rewarded. To have a strong relational culture, it is important to be transparent with your employee growth roadmap. Naturally, most people believe the longer you stay with a company, the more raises you should get. New employees often believe that after a certain amount of time of working at a company, rewards are earned. In contrast, I believe it's important to set expectations with the entire team where rewards are earned through consistent positive results rather than tenure alone. Setting clear expectations for your team communicates how they are able to grow within your organization. It is with this transparency that allows a leader to foster a strong, people-centered culture.

It is also important to have genuine care. Care about your people and care about those around you and spread it to everyone. Make caring for others like an open bottle of water and pour it out on everyone around you. Care can take many forms, from genuinely listening and acknowledging others to taking ownership for failure and giving credit during success. Make care infectious and people will gravitate toward you and your organization. People were made to live in community and when you care and put others first, they will not only gravitate to your organization, but it will also keep them there during the hard times.

There are many examples in the Bible of Jesus demonstrating both effective and caring leadership by putting others before Himself. In His teachings, Jesus both teaches and demonstrates the importance of leading well and being "others" focused. In the Gospel of Luke, Jesus shares the story of the Good Samaritan to a religious leader who came to Him and asked, "What should I do to inherit eternal life?". Jesus asked the religious leader what the law of Moses said to which he replied,

"You must love the Lord your God with all your heart, all your soul, all your strength, and all your mind. And, Love your neighbor as yourself." Jesus was pointing the man first towards God, then towards others. He went on to share the story of the Good Samaritan, which further illustrated the principle of putting others before ourselves. In this lesson, Jesus teaches that leadership is not about us, but instead is about putting God first by serving others.

> "'Love the Lord your God with all your heart and with all your soul and with all your strength and with all your mind'; and, ' Love your neighbor as yourself.'"
> Luke 10:27

To recap, to create a strong, relational culture, you need to 1.) identify your leaders within your team first, 2.) set clear expectations on how your team can grow, and 3.) have a genuine care for others. Ensure your leaders know your core values, have humility, take ownership, and teach decision-making. Ensure your people know and have a clear understanding of how to grow within your company. Finally, ensure you have genuine care for the people around you and put others first. It is infectious.

It's All About Apathy

The Game Plan: Once A Week Caring Habit

Action Item: *Select, Notice, Encourage, Repeat*

Slow is smooth and smooth is fast.

1.) Select *Write it down*

- Select one individual in your personal or professional life (work, school, etc.). This is a person you would like to encourage.

2.) Notice *Seek and listen*

- Intentionally, seek out specific positive behaviors or actions, no matter how small, every time you are around that person.

3.) Encourage *Make it simple yet specific*

- Say a positive, genuine, and encouraging statement to the person.

4.) Repeat *Build genuine trust and stronger relationships*

- Continue this practice and apply it to other individuals in your personal and professional circles. Do this routine once a week.

Example

Once A Week Habit

- Select. You do not know your co-worker Jon very well and you would like to build better rapport.
- Notice. You noticed on several occasions Jon takes out the trash and always leaves the break room clean after use.
- Encourage. The next time you see Jon you say, "Jon, I appreciate how you took out the trash without anyone asking you. That's pretty cool and it really helps the team a lot. Well done!"
- Repeat. Continue this process once a week and apply it with other people in both your personal and professional life. Be intentional when seeking positivity. In the long term, you will build strong relationships and cultivate a culture of genuine care to the people around you. Slow is smooth, and smooth is fast.

Delayed Gratification

CHAPTER FIVE

Delayed Gratification

Both of my parent's families immigrated to the United States from the Philippines when they were children. Their families, like many immigrant families, moved to pursue a better life and escape poverty. Growing up, my parents would tell me stories of their childhood and how they lacked many resources. They told me about the struggles and hardships of poverty and how they pursued and dreamed for success. They wanted what was best for me and they wanted to make sure I would be successful. Based on their life experiences and knowledge, they taught and shared with me many life principles that would help me along my journey in life. I learned many lessons from my parents, but three lessons that stood out to me were being a good steward of my resources, being grateful for the little things, and the concept of delayed gratification.

Stewardship is taking good, responsible care over your resources. These resources can be your money, time, and relationships. We all have limited resources, therefore, it is important to pursue being a good steward to them to help maximize your life.

Gratitude is being thankful and showing appreciation. You need to do this for everything, even the littlest things. It's amazing how much this can change your mindset and attitude.

Start each day with a grateful heart

Delayed gratification is the concept of putting in the work now, so that you can reap the benefits later. It is the idea that instead of taking the short cut and getting the reward right now, you put in the work and take the extra steps, which will ultimately result in a better reward. This is a concept that has played an important role toward the success in my life.

Anything worth having requires hard work and sacrifice. It's also not immediate. As a society, we are losing the ability to think outside of our moment and constantly chasing instant gratification. However, we must step outside of apathetic thinking and instead put intentional thought into what we want out of life. A poverty mentality is thinking for the here and now, whereas a wealth mentality is planning not only for your future, but for future generations.

    When my parents and their families immigrated to America, they came here with a wealth mindset. It required a lot of time and sacrifice, but by taking the path less traveled they not only modeled the lifestyle I wanted, but instilled it in me. They taught me that if you want something different out of life you need to take intentional steps toward changing it. Your results may not be immediate, but they will be worth the wait.

The Game Plan: The Letter

Action Item: *Write a letter addressed to yourself in 1 month.*

It all comes down to your daily decision making

1.) Identify long term goals *Write it down*

- Physical - Where do you want to be physically?
- Mental - Where do you want to be mentally?
- Financial - Where do you want to be financially?
- Spiritual - Where do you want to be spiritually?
- Relational - Where do you want to be relationally?

2.) Think Big Picture *Make long term decisions*

- Map out and visualize the best long term scenario or consequence when making a decision toward your long term goals.
- Ask yourself, "Does this decision now, help with my long term goal?"

3.) Write the letter to yourself *Make the commitment*

- In this letter, write one personal goal and one professional goal you would like to accomplish in 30 days. This letter is just for you. Place it in a spot where you will see it on a daily basis. (I put mine on the fridge!) If you feel comfortable, feel free to share it with others and let them know how they can help you achieve your goals. Repeat this every 30 days!

When you delay instant gratification, you will experience long - term satisfaction!

Just Start Now

CHAPTER SIX

Just Start Now

This is the end of the book. Yes, I know it is short and it may feel rushed, however, I wrote, edited, and published this book all within 30 days and this is the result. A friend of mine made a goal to not only write, but also publish a book within 30 days and challenged me to do the same. I accepted the challenge and we created a 30 day action oriented timeline and established consequences if we did not complete the challenge. From day one, I already knew I would complete the challenge because I had a clear path toward completion and an unfavorable consequence if I did not accomplish it. More importantly though, I established a clear deadline of when the book would be completed.

Parkinson's Law is the saying that "work expands so as to fill the time available for its completion". Basically, this means if you give yourself five weeks to complete a task, it will take you five weeks to complete that task. In the same way, if you give yourself only one week to complete the task, it will take you one week to complete it. The moral of the story is: the closer you set a deadline, the better chance you'll have of completing it by the assigned deadline.

    There are many people out there who have the desire to write their own book and set big, lofty goals with non-committed deadlines. The issue with setting a non-committal deadline is there is a high probability that you'll never actually start the project, and if you do start it, you'll most likely never see the project through to completion. Human nature then takes over and justifies the lack of action with the excuse "I've been really busy" or "I just don't think it is the right time". However, that's not the case. You see, it all comes down to priorities and time management.

    The truth is, with something you truly value, you'll make time for it. Often the most effective and productive people are the ones who have the most tasks to complete and are considered the busiest. Effective people not only value their time, but they are also excellent stewards of their daily schedule. Even with a high work load and busy family life, they often find ways to balance both their personal and professional lives. One common characteristic of a highly effective person is their time management skills. They never procrastinate planning. They always have a clear laid out weekly schedule with all of their important tasks, projects, and deadlines. When new tasks or ideas present themselves, they plan accordingly and start promptly. This brings me to the idea of "Just Start Now". I love the saying, "a year from now, you'll wish you started today." Often times, just starting is half the battle and by simply starting your project, task, or job, you'll greatly increase the chances of getting things done.

Many people say they do not have time to exercise, however, people who make time to exercise often have better work and life balance than those who don't. We all have the time. It simply comes down to what is important and a priority to us.

I'm sure there are many things in your life that you want to accomplish. If you have things you want to get done, I encourage you to identify what these things are and just start now. When you start, "Begin With The End In Mind", which is a habit made famous in the book *The 7 Habits of Highly Effective People* by Stephen Covey. If you want to start a project and see it to completion, you must first carve out time to mentally create a blueprint and visualize the end result. Second, make the decision and commitment that you will follow it through to the end. Third, plan your roadmap. When you plan, it is important to create a deadline date and add it to your calendar. As with Parkinson's Law, give yourself a smaller timeframe than you think you may need. It also helps to create a consequence and add it to your calendar as motivation to complete your project. An example of a consequence for not completing a project could be: taking cold showers everyday at 5AM for the next month or donating $1000 to an organization you dislike and would be embarrassed to share about it with your friends. The key is to find a consequence you would not be happy having to follow through with.

    In the planning phase it is important to break down your project in to smaller, daily tasks and add intentional time in to your calendar to complete these tasks. By breaking down your project in to smaller tasks, you are creating a road map that will lead you to your end goal. Lastly, find an accountability partner to help you keep your pace. This person could be a friend, family member, or co-worker. The main key is to find someone who will not only check in with you regularly, but is willing to hold you accountable through the entire process. There is power in partnership.

Once you have envisioned your end goal and have planned an actionable road map to follow, the next step is simply to "just start now". No more "I'll do it tomorrow" mentality. That type of thinking is apathetic and will get you nowhere in life.

We all have choices in life that we must make. If you are reading this book and have gotten this far, my assumption is you are ready to step outside of a life of apathy. You are ready to move forward with intentional thinking and take the actionable steps necessary to achieve your goals. Although the process will feel uncomfortable, and challenge not only your thinking, but also your daily habits I encourage you to push through. You did not get where you are overnight and you will not change who you are overnight. So, you must assess your value system: determine what is most important to you in terms of goals and then apply these six principles to go after them. Remember, to receive more, you have to be willing to put in more, which means it's going to take work. And a lot of it.

It's time to step out of apathy and make some moves! It's going to stretch and grow you in ways you didn't know were possible, but I promise you it will be worth it. The real change takes place once you start living intentionally, and not apathetically.

So, what are you waiting for? It's time to make some moves!

The Game Plan: Just Start Now

Action Item: *Visualize, Plan, Start*

Choose a project or goal you would like to get done

1.) Begin With The End In Mind *Write it down*

- Visualize what you would like the end result to look like
- Make the decision and commit to complete your project

2.) Plan *Build your roadmap*

- When will you complete the project? *Choose a deadline within 30 and 60 days*
- What is your consequence for failure? *Choose something you strongly dislike*
- What does your daily task timeline look like? *Add daily action items to your calendar that add toward your goal*
- Who is your accountability partner? *Find someone who will hold you accountable to your timeline*

3.) Start *Right Now*

- Don't wait. Start making moves and hold yourself accountable

It's All About Apathy